DISCOV PENGUINS

by Helen Foster James

Cherry Lake Publishing • Ann Arbor, Michigan

3

Published in the United States of America
by Cherry Lake Publishing
Ann Arbor, Michigan
www.cherrylakepublishing.com

Content Adviser: William McLellan, research associate, Center for Marine Science, University of North Carolina, Wilmington
Reading Adviser: Marla Conn, ReadAbility, Inc

Photo Credits: © Stanislav Fosenbauer/Shutterstock Images, cover; © prochasson Frederic/Shutterstock Images, 4; © Natalia Pushchina/Shutterstock Images, 6; © InnaFelker/Shutterstock Images, 8; © Eric Isselee/Shutterstock Images, 10; © Volt Collection/Shutterstock Images, 12; © Volodymyr Goinyk/ Shutterstock Images, 14; © Armin Rose/Shutterstock Images, 16; © Brendan Van Son/Shutterstock Images, 18; © Fredy Theurig/Shutterstock Images, 20

Library of Congress Cataloging-in-Publication Data
James, Helen Foster, 1951- author.
  Discover penguins / Helen Foster James.
      pages cm.—(Splash!)
  Summary: "This Level 3 guided reader introduces basic facts about penguins, including their physical characteristics, diet, and habitat. Simple callouts ask the student to think in new ways, supporting inquiry-based reading. Additional text features and search tools, including a glossary and an index, help students locate information and learn new words."— Provided by publisher.
  Audience: Ages 6–10
  Audience: K to grade 3
  Includes bibliographical references and index.
  ISBN 978-1-63362-603-4 (hardcover)—ISBN 978-1-63362-693-5 (pbk.)— ISBN 978-1-63362-783-3 (pdf)—ISBN 978-1-63362-873-1 (ebook)
  1. Penguins—Juvenile literature. I. Title.

QL696.S47J36 2016
598.47—dc23

                                        2014048655

Cherry Lake Publishing would like to acknowledge the work of The Partnership for 21st Century Skills. Please visit www.p21.org for more information.

Printed in the United States of America
Corporate Graphics

TABLE OF CONTENTS

Penguins Love a Crowd

Penguins are birds but can't fly. They walk **upright** when on land. They **waddle** when they walk. Their wings are **flippers** they use to swim. They are fast swimmers.

Penguins can't fly, but they swim very well.

Not all penguins are alike. Emperor penguins are the tallest **species** of penguins. Little blues are the smallest species.

THINK!

How do you think people learn about penguins?
Where can you go to learn more about penguins?

These little blue penguins are the smallest type of penguin.

Penguins like to be with other penguins. They swim, feed, and nest in groups.

 These black-footed penguins live in South Africa.

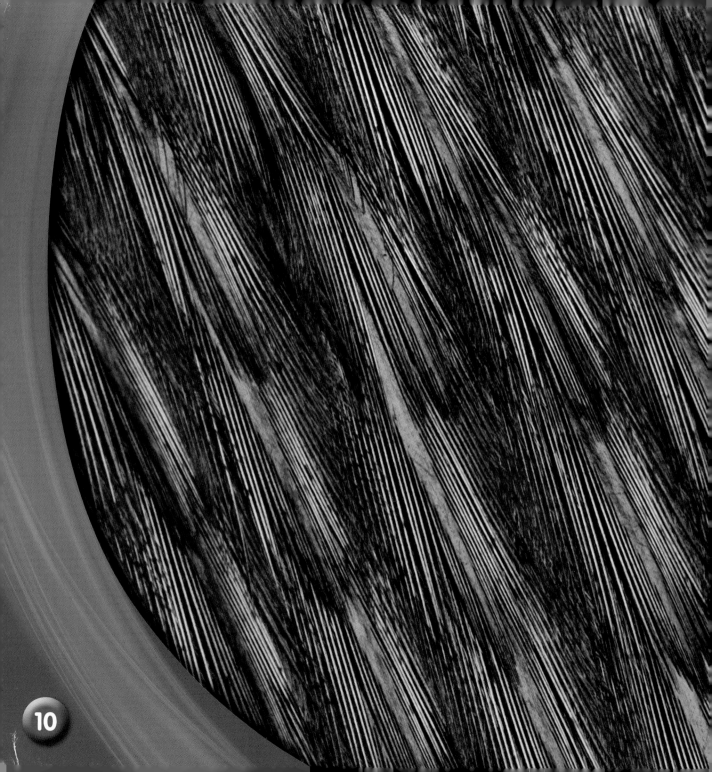

Growing Up in the Cold

Penguins have more feathers than most birds. The feathers are close to each other. Because they **overlap**, the feathers trap air on the inner layer and keep the penguins warm.

A penguin's layer of feathers keeps it warm.

Their black and white coloring helps keep them safe from **predators**. Penguins **molt** once a year. They replace their old feathers with new ones.

LOOK!

Some people say it looks like penguins wear tuxedos. Why do you think they say this?

This emperor penguin is molting.

Penguin mothers and fathers both take care of the eggs. In some species, the father holds the egg on his feet. This keeps the egg warm. The egg hatches in one to two months. A penguin parent knows its chick by the call it makes!

This penguin chick needs food from its parents.

Penguins use their flippers
and feet to slide down snowy hills.
This is called **tobogganing**.

These emperor penguins are tobogganing.

Protecting Penguins

Earth's climate is getting warmer. This creates a problem. Some penguins can't live without ice. People around the world work to protect penguins.

Scientists have studied penguins on land. Scientists hope to learn more about what penguins do in the ocean.

If Earth keeps getting warmer, penguins will be in danger.

January 20 is Penguin Awareness Day. April 25 is World Penguin Day. People pay special attention to penguins on these days. Learning about penguins will help keep them safe.

CREATE! Draw a picture of three types of penguins. Label them and tell how they are different from each other.

These are rockhopper penguins.

Think About It

Why do you think scientists know less about what penguins do when they are in the ocean than what they do on land?

How might a warmer climate hurt penguins? Go online with an adult to research this.

Find Out More

BOOK

Gray, Susan H. *Penguins Can't Fly*. Ann Arbor, MI: Cherry Lake Publishing, 2014.

WEB SITE

Aquarium of the Pacific—Penguin Habitat
www.aquariumofpacific.org/exhibits/penguin_habitat
Learn about penguins, and watch them below and above water on their webcams.

National Geographic Kids—Animals: Emperor Penguin
http://kids.nationalgeographic.com/content/kids/en_US/animals/emperor-penguin/
Find information about emperor penguins at this site.

Glossary

flippers (FLIP-urz) broad, flat body parts, such as arms or legs, that sea creatures use to swim

molt (MOHLT) to lose old feathers so that new ones can grow

overlap (oh-vur-LAP) to extend over or partly cover something

predators (PRED-uh-turz) animals that live by hunting other animals to eat

species (SPEE-sheez) one type, or kind, of plant or animal

tobogganing (tuh-BAH-guhn-ing) sliding downhill on ice or snow

upright (UHP-rite) standing straight up; vertical

waddle (WAH-duhl) to walk by taking short steps and moving slightly from side to side

Index

About the Author

Dr. Helen Foster James likes to read, travel, and volunteer as a naturalist interpreter in the mountains. She has traveled to see Humboldt penguins on an island off the coast of Peru. She lives in San Diego, California, with her husband, Bob.